HOW
Do I Teach This Kid?

Visual Work Tasks for Beginning Learners on the Autism Spectrum

Kimberly A. Henry

How Do I Teach This Kid?

All marketing and publishing rights guaranteed to and reserved by

FUTURE HORIZONS INC.

721 W. Abram Street
Arlington, Texas 76013
800-489-0727
817-277-0727
817-277-2270 (fax)
E-mail: info@FHautism.com
www.FHautism.com

Cover design and book layout:
Matt Mitchell, www.mattmitchelldesign.com

ISBN 10: 1-932565-24-8
ISBN 13: 978-1-932565-24-9

Table of Contents

Acknowledgements vii

About this Resource ix

What are task boxes? xi

Creating an independent work system xvi

Stuff to save for task boxes xvii

What do you do with the stuff once you get it? xix

Tricks and tips for task box construction...................... xxi

Task boxes to make

Motor tasks 1

    Put blocks in slot 3

    Pull clothespins off box, put in hole 4

    Put mini balls in hole 5

    Pull blocks off box, put in hole 6

    Pull teddy bears off box 7

    Put big checkers in slot.. 8

    Park cars in spot 9

    Assemble film canisters and drop in slot................ 10

    Put poker chips in slot 11

    Put coins in bank 12

    Put facial features on a potato toy 13

    Block construction 14

Matching tasks 15

    Plastic egg color match 17

Clothespin color match 18

Puzzle piece outline match 19

Blocks color match 20

Tile sample color match 21

Simple picture match 22

Match block pattern 23

Memory match 24

Shape match...25

Border picture match 26

Box top match 27

Object to photo match 28

Lotto picture match 29

Sorting tasks 31

2-color car sort...33

3-color poker chip sort 34

4-color game piece sort...35

3-way colored beads sort 36

Colored straw sort 37

Boy-girl sort..38

Teddy bear color sort 39

Sports eraser sort..40

Balls and blocks sort 41

Ghosts and pumpkins sort 42

Apples and pumpkins sort 43

Paint card sort 44

Crayon sort 45

Plastic utensils sort 46

Sort sports cards by category 47

File index cards by color...................................48

Same/different sort..49

Texture sort 50

Category sort 51

Sort by size 52

Reading tasks 53

Alphabet sequence 55

Upper-to-lower case letter match....................56

Word-to-word match 57

Word-to-picture match......................................58

Clothespin word-to-picture match 59

Blocks-to-color words match 60

Paperclips-to-color words match 61

Sentence-to-picture match 62

Initial sound sort 63

Initial letter match 64

Character and setting sort 65

3-part story sequence 66

File by first letter..67

File words by category 68

Alphabetical order on clothespins 69

Holiday-to-month name binder 70

Opposites binder 71

Writing tasks 73

Trace lines 75

Draw lines to match 76

Spell name sequence 77

Letter match to spell word 78

Attach clothespins to spell words 79

Simple sentence construction with pictures 80

Simple sentence construction with words 81

Math tasks 83

1:1 correspondence with pegs and film canisters 85

1:1 correspondence with cotton balls and ice cube tray .. 86

Count dots, match to number 87

Count sets of items, match to number 88

Sequence numbers on strip 89

Make sets on a box 90

Fill in the sequence with missing number 91

Sequence by skip counting 92

Size seriation 93

Make sets in ice cube tray 94

Make sets in cups 95

Extend pattern with stickers 96

Appendix I: Sample IEP goals 97

Appendix II: Data sheets for tracking independence 103

Acknowledgements

Over the years, the work of many has contributed to wonderful advancements in the lives of autistic children and those close to them. Ms. Kimberly Henry and Future Horizons would like to accredit and extend personal gratitude to several entities and outstanding individuals that have, through their hard work, laid the foundation for *How Do I Teach This Kid*:

North Carolina's TEACCH program
http://www.teacch.com/

Laurie Eckenrode, Pat Fennell, and Kathy Hearsey,
creators of Tasks Galore
http://www.tasksgalore.com

Ron and Linda Larsen of Centering on Children, Inc.,
creators of ShoeboxTasks
http://www.shoeboxtasks.com

We hope that our readers will utilize these resources, too, as we work to improve the lives of people touched by autism.

Credit is also given to Ginna Drahan for use of her photographs of Raimee, one of my first students with autism, on the chapter divider pages.

About this Resource

Students with developmental delays such as those on the autistic spectrum often need direct instruction to learn to stay on task and complete assignments independently. The ideas presented in this book are designed to increase the independent work skills of beginning-level learners. The tasks are designed as starting points for students who are learning how to work independently. The visual work task system described in this book can be used by anyone teaching a child to become more independent: special education teachers, parents, and home-based therapists. The tasks can be used with preschoolers through adolescents. The tasks can even be incorporated into work times within general education classrooms. Work systems help provide students with the skills and task commitment to work independently for a sustained period of time. Students who can work independently and maintain attention to several tasks in a row typically experience a higher rate of success, both at school and in the work force.

Ideas for over 80 independent work tasks are presented in this practical resource. Each task description includes a photograph and a detailed list of materials needed to create the task. Suggestions for differentiating the task to meet the needs of learners at different levels are also included with each idea. Introductory material describes work tasks in more detail and suggests ways to establish an independent work system for your student. The Appendix contains sample goals for reflecting a student's need for developing independent work skills in an Individual Education Plan (IEP). The Appendix also includes sample data sheets for tracking student progress with the work tasks.

Much research has been done that shows that children with autism are strong visual learners. Additionally, children with autism thrive on routine, consistency and clear expectations. Task boxes provide visual cues to enable students to work independently of adults—to derive from the task what is to be done and when it is to be finished. Teaching a child to work independently through a work system of task boxes allows them to use this need for routine and consistency to learn new skills and achieve success. Most importantly, however, task boxes enable a child to develop independence—the ultimate goal of any educational program.

What Are Task Boxes?

Task boxes are single, organized activities with a clear beginning and end. All task materials are contained within clearly defined boundaries—trays, boxes, baskets, tubs, folders, binders. Each task is presented with visual organization and clarity. The materials clearly define the activity for the student and tell him how to complete the task. For example, one task may have four cups —one red, one green, one blue, and one yellow—pushed through holes cut in the top of a shoebox, and a container of red, green, blue, and yellow blocks attached to the side of the box. The organization of the task shows the child that he is to sort the blocks by color and place them in the corresponding cups. Additionally, the organization of the task itself teaches the concept of "finished" since the student knows that the task is completed when all of the materials have been used.

Task boxes emphasize students' visual learning styles, avoiding the need for auditory processing of verbal directions, an area of deficit for many students with autism. The manipulative nature of task boxes provides students with tactile and kinesthetic activities; however, the visual structure and organization of the manipulatives prevents stereotypical spinning, tossing, or stimming with the materials since students can "see" the task to be completed.

The task boxes presented in this resource address six different skill areas: motor tasks, matching, sorting, reading, writing, and math. Motor task boxes are the first step for many children who are just learning to work independently. Skills such as "pulling off" and "putting in" are presented in a visual format to make the task expectation clear to the child. The concept of "finished" is taught by showing the child that the task is finished when all of the materials are gone.

Matching and sorting task boxes are useful for students who have visual discrimination skills and are able to recognize items as being the same or different. Various materials can be used to teach students to match and sort colors, pictures, shapes, and objects. Higher level skills such as sorting by category and filing can also be presented in task box format.

Beginning academic skills in reading, writing, and math can be taught through the use of task boxes. Students can follow a visual structure to sequence letters and numbers, place words in alphabetical order, construct a simple sentence, spell words, demonstrate one-to-one correspondence, extend a pattern—the possibilities are endless! All you need is a little creativity, some organizational containers, and a few manipulatives that you either find or create. You can tailor task boxes to the individual needs of one student or create them to be used by multiple students at different levels.

Initially, the tasks are usually taught within structured teaching sessions and then incorporated into an independent work system as students develop proficiency. Once students have mastered the tasks of three or four boxes, begin to transfer them to an independent work system.

Creating A Work System

Like task boxes, work systems capitalize on students' visual strengths and can be tailored to the unique abilities of the child. A work system teaches a child what and how much work is to be completed and when it is finished. To achieve these goals, a work system follows the same principles as work tasks: visual organization and visual clarity. Tasks to be completed are presented in a systematic fashion with minimal distractors or irrelevant material. When a work system is first introduced, direct instruction must occur to teach a child how to follow the system—how to get the tasks, complete them, and where to put them when they are finished.

In a structured work system, work routinely flows from left to right. Tasks to be completed are placed on the student's left. One task at a time is brought to the work surface, completed, and then transferred to a "finished" area to the student's right. It is often helpful to have a shelving unit on the left of the student to hold the tasks to be completed in an organized fashion. Shelves for finished tasks may also be on the right of the student. However, some people prefer to use a laundry basket or other large container for finished work. The child completes the work and then places it in the "finished basket" on the floor to his right. One example of this type of work system organization is depicted in the photo on the next page:

A schedule of work to be completed may also assist some students in finishing the tasks independently. The schedule should match coding on the task boxes—colors, letters, numbers, pictures, etc. A schedule strip can be mounted to the work surface in front of the child. The schedule defines the order in which the child is to complete the tasks on his left. For example, a schedule strip may contain a green square of paper, a red square, and a yellow square, attached to the strip with Velcro®. Each box to be completed has a matching green, red, or yellow square on the outside of the box. The child will remove the first colored square, match it to the outside of the box with the same color square and then complete the task in the box. A piece of loop-Velcro® is placed on the colored square. The photo on the next page illustrates an example of a schedule strip with cards to be matched to the outside of the task box.

The goal of organized work systems is for the student to complete the tasks independently—without any prompting or assistance from another person. Tasks are only placed in the work system when the child can complete them independently. Work systems can begin with only one or two tasks if that is the independent performance level of the child. As the child becomes more proficient, the number and complexity of the tasks can increase.

Task boxes are easy to make out of materials you already have or can find around the house. On the following page is a letter that you can use to ask people to save task box items for you.

Dear Teachers,

As you clean out your rooms at the end of the year (and clean out your children's rooms at home, too!), could you save any of the following items that you find and no longer need:

❏ shoe boxes with lids
❏ ice cube trays
❏ egg cartons
❏ jewelry boxes (earring or necklace size)
❏ coffee cans with plastic lids
❏ peanut cans with lids
❏ empty Playdoh cans with lids
❏ soft-drink-can flats
❏ plastic strawberry baskets
❏ old Memory games, Bingo games (missing pieces ok!)
❏ spare pieces from games
❏ groups of objects to sort
❏ blocks
❏ Legos
❏ pop beads
❏ plastic links
❏ wooden puzzles (even stray pieces are ok)
❏ sports cards
❏ calendars with pictures
❏ Disney catalogs
❏ clothespins
❏ board books
❏ dried out markers with the tops
❏ plastic spice jars with lids
❏ plastic yogurt, applesauce, butter, cottage cheese, etc. containers

Please give to _____. Thanks!

What do you do with this stuff once you get it?

These items can be used as containers for tasks:

- ☑ shoe boxes with lids
- ☑ ice cube trays
- ☑ egg cartons
- ☑ jewelry boxes (earring or necklace size)
- ☑ coffee cans with plastic lids
- ☑ peanut cans with lids
- ☑ empty Playdoh cans with lids
- ☑ soft-drink-can flats
- ☑ plastic strawberry baskets
- ☑ plastic spice jars with lids
- ☑ plastic yogurt, applesauce, butter, cottage cheese, etc. containers

These items can be used as manipulatives in the tasks:

- ☑ old Memory games, Bingo games (missing pieces ok!)— could be used for matching tasks
- ☑ spare pieces from games—could be used to sort by color, sort by item, items to count or make sets with, etc.
- ☑ groups of objects to sort—could be used to sort by item, to match item to picture of item, to match item to written word of item, to sort by initial sound of the item, to sort by color

☑ blocks—could be used to sort by color, to match block to color word, to make patterns, to count or make sets

☑ Legos—could be used to sort by color, to sort by size or shape, to assemble a structure like a model

☑ pop beads—could be used to pull apart and put in a container with a lid

☑ plastic links—could be used to sort by color, to extend a pattern, to count or make sets

☑ puzzles—could be used as objects are—to match the puzzle piece to a picture of the item on the piece, to match the puzzle piece picture to the written word, to sort by initial sound of the picture on the puzzle piece

☑ sports cards—to sort by sport, to file by sport, to file by last name

☑ calendars with pictures—to match smaller thumbnail picture (usually found on the back of the calendar) to the larger calendar page

☑ Disney catalogs—I often use the photos as motivational materials for making task boxes—kids like to match pictures of Mickey Mouse, Pooh, etc.

☑ clothespins—to use with motor tasks—pull off the side of a box, pinch and put on the side of a box, write on the clothespins and match to the corresponding spot on cardboard

☑ board books—could be adapted with Velcro® to use in matching or reading tasks

☑ dried-out markers with the tops—can use as a motor task—assembling the correct top on the marker; or as a color sorting task with just the tops, or as objects to count, make sets with

Tricks and Tips for Task Box Construction

Use a consistent system for placing Velcro® on your task boxes. Usually, the hook (or scratchy) Velcro® is placed on the manipulatives and the loop (or soft) Velcro® is placed on the box. A simple mnemonic is "hook in the hand" and "soft on the surface." Consistent placement will allow you to interchange materials with other task boxes.

Use a utility knife or scissors to cut an X in the top of a coffee can or other container to provide a little resistance for motor tasks. Additionally, some children enjoy the sensory input provided by the plastic as they push the item through the hole.

Tasks can be changed to meet the needs of many students or to utilize different materials with the same task box. Instead of permanently attaching items to the top of the shoebox, clear adhesive photo corners can be attached to the box and the picture can be removed and changed to allow a different task to be presented using the same box. Photo corners can be purchased wherever photo albums and supplies are sold or at many craft stores in the scrapbooking department.

When using egg cartons for tasks, an easy way to differentiate is to alter the number of spots in the egg carton. Paper egg cartons can be cut in half to provide only 6 spots to be filled with items. Some egg cartons even hold 24 eggs—allowing lots of practice in the task!

The small containers that hold the loose manipulatives or work to be completed can be attached to the larger shoebox with Velcro® to make the entire task box one contained unit. This helps ensure that when the child gets the task box off of the shelf, he gets all parts and the task expectations are clear.

The schedule of work to be completed can be arranged either horizontally or vertically, depending on personal preference. Sometimes it seems that a vertical schedule is easier to follow. If you find that your student does not complete the work in the order that the schedule dictates, and you are using a schedule system of colors, shapes, or pictures to be matched to the task box, you may want to try using letters or numbers. I have found that if I place 1,2,3 or A,B,C on a schedule strip, the students usually complete the work in that order since many of my students tend to enjoy the correct sequence of letters and numbers and don't like them to be out of order.

If a task involves the student dropping items in several different holes in the box and you want to be able to check for correctness after the task is completed, create dividers inside the box that will allow you to see whether all items were dropped in the correct holes.

To extend a sequencing task such as sequencing numbers or letters, simply make two or more strips that you can join together to make the task longer. Put hook-Velcro® on the back of the right end of the first strip and loop-Velcro® on the top of the left end of the second strip. Fasten them together and you have more work to be done!

To extend the life of the materials in your tasks, you may wish to laminate them for extra durability. Even if you don't have a heat laminator available to you, office supply stores sell cool or press-on lamination that works just as well.

As always, be cautious of the age and tendencies of your students. Do not use manipulatives that are very small with young children or children who have a tendency to place items in their mouths.

To keep all of your task boxes organized, be sure to write on the ends of the boxes what tasks they contain. That way you will be able to find the box you need quickly.

MOTOR
TASKS

TASK:
The student will place blocks in a slot.

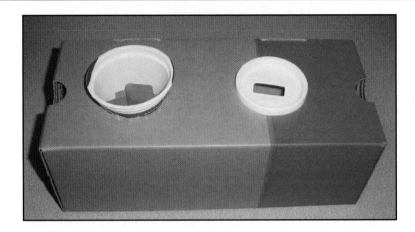

MATERIALS:
- ❑ thin rectangular or square blocks
- ❑ 2 plastic cups or containers, one with a lid with a slit cut into it (the slit should be just big enough to fit the blocks in)
- ❑ a shoebox with a lid and two holes cut into it to hold the containers

TARGETED SKILLS:
- ❑ fine-motor
- ❑ eye-hand coordination

IDEAS FOR DIFFERENTIATION:
The task could be expanded by putting 2 differently shaped blocks (e.g., squares and circles) in the left container and adding another cup with a slit that matches the second shape. Students would have to place the correct block in the slot that matches its shape.

Different color blocks of the same shape could be used with a second cup with a slit. Each cup's lid would be color coded to match the two colors of blocks. Students would sort the blocks by color and place them in the correct slot.

TASK:
The student will remove clothespins from the box and place in the hole.

MATERIALS:
- ❏ 10-15 clothespins (number can vary depending on student's skill level and endurance)
- ❏ a container with a small hole cut in the top to insert the clothespins
- ❏ a shoebox to contain all materials

TARGETED SKILLS:
- ❏ fine-motor (pincer grasp)
- ❏ eye-hand coordination

IDEAS FOR DIFFERENTIATION:
For students unable to remove clothespins using a pincer grasp, the clothespins could be placed in a separate tub. The student would simply take a clothespin from the tub and place it in the hole in the other container.

TASK:
The student will put mini balls in a hole.

MATERIALS:
- ❏ several small balls (these should be textured balls like mini-Koosh balls to provide some sensory input)
- ❏ a container with a lid with an "X" slit cut in the top
- ❏ a tray or box to contain all materials

TARGETED SKILLS:
- ❏ fine-motor
- ❏ eye-hand coordination

CONSTRUCTION TIP:
Cutting an "X" in the top of the plastic lid provides some tactile sensory input. The student has to push with a little bit of force to get the ball in the hole and many students like the feel of pushing their fingers into the "X" as they release the ball. (see page xix for a close-up picture of the lid)

TASK:
The student will pull blocks off and place in the hole.

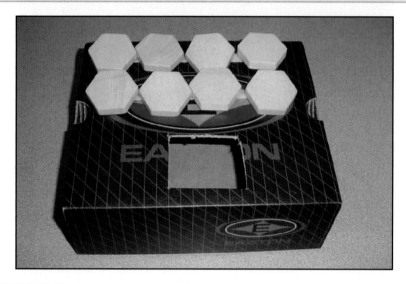

MATERIALS:
- ❏ blocks with hook-Velcro® squares on the back
- ❏ a shoebox with a hole cut in the lid and loop-Velcro® strips on top of the box above the hole

TARGETED SKILLS:
- ❏ fine-motor

IDEAS FOR DIFFERENTIATION:
Any number of different items may replace the blocks to utilize student interests and build motivation for the task (plastic dinosaurs, jingle bells, etc.).

TASK:
The student will pull plastic teddy bear counters from a box and drop into a container.

MATERIALS:
- ❏ teddy bear counters (sold at teacher supply stores and some toy stores) or other plastic manipulatives with hook-Velcro® on the bottom of each object
- ❏ a small container in which to drop the bears
- ❏ a shoebox with pieces of loop-Velcro® attached to the left side of the lid and a hole cut in the right side of the lid to hold the small container

TARGETED SKILLS:
- ❏ fine-motor

IDEAS FOR DIFFERENTIATION:
Students could also complete this task in reverse: take the bears out of the container and attach to the Velcro® on top of the box. This would work on one-to-one correspondence as well as fine-motor skills. Be sure to turn the box around so that the child is still working from left to right. For some students, you may need to use different materials or create a different box when expecting them to complete the reverse task.

TASK:
The student will put checkers in a slot.

MATERIALS:
- ❏ checkers (these extra large ones are sold at some dollar stores)
- ❏ a container to hold the checkers
- ❏ a shoebox with a slot matching the thickness of the checkers

TARGETED SKILLS:
- ❏ fine-motor

IDEAS FOR DIFFERENTIATION:
Different-sized checkers could be used within this task to work on size discrimination as well as the fine-motor skill of placing them through the slot. Be sure to cut two slots in the box, one that only the small checkers will fit through and one that the large checkers will fit through. Be sure to create a checking system inside the box to assess the student's accuracy since the small checkers will fit through the large hole also (see tip on page xxi).

TASK:
The student will "park" cars on top of a box.

MATERIALS:

❏ toy cars with hook-Velcro® on the bottom of each car

❏ a small container to hold the cars

❏ a shoebox (could be decorated as a "road") with pieces of loop-Velcro® attached to the top of the box for "parking spots"

TARGETED SKILLS:

❏ motor

❏ one-to-one correspondence

IDEAS FOR DIFFERENTIATION:

The loop-Velcro® could be colored with a marker to correspond to the different color cars. Students could then match the correct color car to its corresponding colored "parking spot".

TASK:
The student will assemble film canisters and drop in slot.

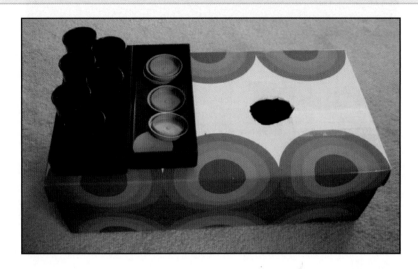

MATERIALS:
- ❏ a small container holding film canisters
- ❏ a small container holding film canister lids
- ❏ hook-Velcro® strips attached to the bottom of the small containers
- ❏ a shoebox with with loop-Velcro® strips on top to affix the small containers and one hole in which to drop the assembled canisters

TARGETED SKILLS:
- ❏ fine-motor
- ❏ two-step tasks

IDEAS FOR DIFFERENTIATION:
A third step could be added to this assembly task by having the student place an item such as a cotton ball inside the canister before attaching the lid and dropping in the slot.

TASK:
The student will place poker chips in different types of slots.

MATERIALS:

- ❏ 3 different-colored poker chips and a container to hold them
- ❏ a shoebox with different slot orientations cut into the box for the students to drop the chips in

TARGETED SKILLS:

- ❏ fine-motor
- ❏ pincer grasp
- ❏ eye-hand coordination; color-matching could be embedded if the chips are to be sorted and placed in the slots by color (as pictured in the task above).

CONSTRUCTION TIP:

You may wish to design a checking system for the inside of the box to be certain that all the white chips went in vertically, the blue chips went in horizontally, etc. (see page xxi for photo of this tip). However, this task is more about the motor skill than color sorting and it may not matter to you which chips went in which hole as long as the child is using all three types of slots for a motor challenge.

TASK:
The student will put coins in a bank.

MATERIALS:
- ❏ various plastic coins
- ❏ a small container to hold the coins
- ❏ a bank or other small container with a slit in the lid
- ❏ a container to hold all materials

TARGETED SKILLS:
- ❏ fine-motor
- ❏ pincer grasp
- ❏ eye-hand coordination

CONSTRUCTION TIP:
Be sure that the size of the coins is appropriate for your students. You want to be cautious about using small items if your students tend to place things in their mouths.

TASK:
The student will put facial features on a potato toy.

MATERIALS:
- ❏ a potato toy
- ❏ a small container to hold the facial features of the potato toy
- ❏ a container to hold the potato toy as it is assembled

TARGETED SKILLS:
- ❏ fine-motor
- ❏ eye-hand coordination; some body part recognition if correct placement is an identified target

IDEAS FOR DIFFERENTIATION:
Vary the number and kinds of features that are to be placed on the potato toy. There are many different kinds of potato toys on the market today (potato pirates, potato kids, etc.) that could be used with this task.

TASK:
The student will construct a block structure using interlocking blocks.

MATERIALS:
- ❏ several colors of interlocking blocks and a container to hold them
- ❏ a model of a completed block structure affixed to the top of a shoe box
- ❏ (once the child has built the structure, the finished product can be placed back in the empty container where the loose blocks were contained)

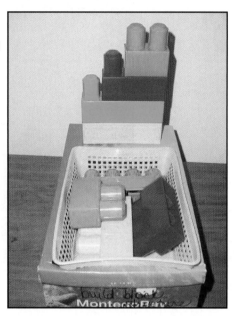

TARGETED SKILLS:
- ❏ fine-motor
- ❏ eye-hand coordination

IDEAS FOR DIFFERENTIATION:
You can vary the complexity of the task by using different-sized or -shaped blocks. Be sure to have blocks that match exactly the ones used in the model structures.

CONSTRUCTION TIP:
You may wish to use hot glue to permanently attach the blocks in your model structure so that students will not pull it apart or use the pieces to create their structure.

MATCHING TASKS

TASK:
The student will match plastic colored eggs to corresponding spots in an egg carton.

MATERIALS:
- ❏ colored plastic eggs
- ❏ egg carton
- ❏ colored sticker dots placed in each spot in the egg carton

TARGETED SKILLS:
- ❏ matching
- ❏ math readiness

IDEAS FOR DIFFERENTIATION:
Eggs could be broken apart and students could assemble them prior to matching to the correct color for additional fine-motor work.

The color word could be written on a white sticker and placed in the bottom of the egg carton and the student could match the egg to the correct color word.

TASK:
The student will match clothespins to corresponding colors.

MATERIALS:

❑ colored clothespins

❑ cardboard squares color coded to match clothespin colors

❑ a container to hold the clothespins

❑ a tray or container to hold all items

TARGETED SKILLS:

❑ matching

❑ math readiness

❑ fine-motor

IDEAS FOR DIFFERENTIATION:

For a simpler, shorter task, place only one of each color clothespin in the container. Students will finish with only one clothespin on each cardboard square.

Instead of color coding by drawing with marker on the cardboard, each square could have the color word written on it and students could place the clothespins on the cardboard at the correct color word.

TASK:
The student will match shaped items to shape outlines.

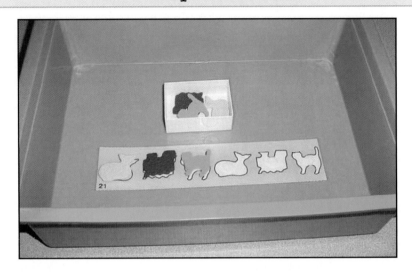

MATERIALS:
- ❏ various small items with distinct shapes with hook-Velcro® on each back
- ❏ a cardboard strip with the outlines of each item traced onto the cardboard and small pieces of loop-Velcro® in the center of each outline
- ❏ a container to hold the items to be matched
- ❏ a tray or container to hold all items

TARGETED SKILLS:
- ❏ matching
- ❏ visual discrimination
- ❏ math readiness

CONSTRUCTION TIP:
Do you have inlay or knob puzzles that are missing pieces? This task can utilize the pieces you do have. Rather than placing the pieces in the formboard, trace their outlines on cardboard, attach some Velcro®, and you have a new use for those incomplete puzzles!

TASK:
The student will match colored blocks to colored spots in an ice tray.

MATERIALS:

- ❏ colored one-inch blocks
- ❏ a container to hold the blocks
- ❏ an ice tray or egg carton with colored sticker dots in each spot that correspond with the colors of the blocks
- ❏ a shoe box lid or tray to hold all of the materials

TARGETED SKILLS:

- ❏ matching
- ❏ math readiness
- ❏ 1:1 correspondence

IDEAS FOR DIFFERENTIATION:

For a shorter task, use an egg carton and cut it in half. The student will then only need to match colors in six spots instead of twelve.

To work on one-to-one correspondence without the matching component, remove the stickers from the ice tray and use only one color block. With these materials, the student needs to place one block in each spot on the tray.

TASK:
The student will match colored tiles.

MATERIALS:

❏ colored tiles (those pictured are free samples of kitchen countertops and may often be obtained at home improvement stores); the tiles are usually hanging on display in the store and already have holes punched in them

❏ a small container to hold the tiles

❏ a shoe box with plastic, self-adhesive hooks on which to hang the tiles

❏ samples of each color tile affixed to the shoe box for a visual model of the task

TARGETED SKILLS:

❏ matching

❏ math readiness

❏ fine-motor

CONSTRUCTION TIP:

Plastic hooks can be attached to a sturdy piece of cardboard instead of a shoebox for a smaller task "box." Model tiles can be affixed to the shoebox with hot glue or other strong adhesive.

TASK:
The student will match identical, simple pictures.

MATERIALS:
- ❏ 2 sets of pictures that are grossly dissimilar to each other (those pictured are sold in teacher stores as tags used for marking the dates on a calendar)
- ❏ a shoebox with a lid with one set of the pictures attached along a top row and one piece of loop-Velcro® underneath each picture
- ❏ a container to hold the loose pictures

TARGETED SKILLS:
- ❏ matching
- ❏ visual discrimination
- ❏ pre-reading

CONSTRUCTION TIP:
To change the pictures on this task box without having to make a new box, attach clear adhesive photo corners to the pictures before placing them on the top row of the box. When you need to remove the pictures and put different ones in, simply take the picture out of the photo corners. The corners will stay on the box and different pictures can be inserted (see page xix for close-up photo of this tip).

TASK:
The student will match same colored blocks in a predetermined pattern.

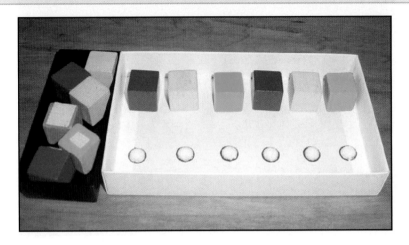

MATERIALS:
- ❏ a shoebox with one-inch colored blocks affixed in a single row on the top of the shoebox lid
- ❏ loop-Velcro® dots in a second row, one below each affixed block
- ❏ loose blocks with hook-Velcro® on the bottoms identical to those on the shoebox lid
- ❏ a small container to hold the loose blocks

TARGETED SKILLS:
- ❏ matching
- ❏ math readiness

CONSTRUCTION TIP:
Hot glue could be used to affix the top row of blocks to the shoebox lid. This will create a permanent bond and will reduce confusion that might occur if all the blocks have Velcro® on them. Also, when affixing white Velcro® to a white surface, it helps to outline or color in the Velcro® with a dark marker to make the Velcro® stand out for the student.

TASK:
The student will match detailed pictures.

MATERIALS:
- ❏ pairs of pictures to be matched (those pictured are from a Memory game)
- ❏ a tray to hold the matched pairs (again, this tray comes with a Memory game)
- ❏ a container to hold all of the pictures to be matched

TARGETED SKILLS:
- ❏ matching
- ❏ visual discrimination
- ❏ pre-reading

CONSTRUCTION TIP:
You may wish to tape or glue one of each picture to the bottom of the tray. That way, the picture to be matched stays in the tray and the child's task is to place the loose picture on top of its match in the tray.

TASK:
The student will match shapes.

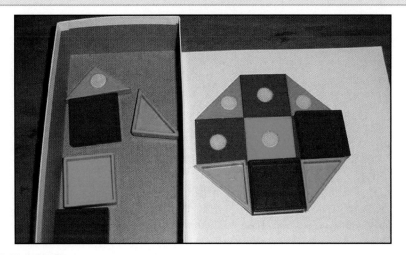

MATERIALS:
- ❏ assorted loose shape blocks with hook-Velcro® in the center of each shape
- ❏ a traced and colored design on the top of a shoebox or piece of cardboard that uses the loose shapes
- ❏ loop-Velcro® in the center of each shape on the design
- ❏ a small container to hold the loose shapes

TARGETED SKILLS:
- ❏ matching
- ❏ math readiness

IDEAS FOR DIFFERENTIATION:
The same shapes could also be used for a sorting task. Students could sort all triangles, circles, squares, etc.

CONSTRUCTION TIP:
When creating the design, be sure to use each shape only once. The student needs to match all the shapes in the box in order to be finished. Try to color the design so that it looks as much like the loose shapes as possible.

TASK:
The student will match pictures on a border strip.

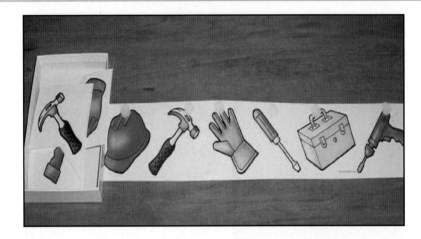

MATERIALS:
- ❏ a strip with different pictures on it (the example pictured above uses 2 identical strips of commercially available bulletin board border)
- ❏ pieces of loop-Velcro® placed above each picture
- ❏ identical pictures, cut into individual pieces with hook-Velcro® on the backs
- ❏ a container to hold the loose pictures

TARGETED SKILLS:
- ❏ matching
- ❏ math readiness
- ❏ reading readiness

CONSTRUCTION TIP:
Many bulletin board borders have simple, discrete pictures running the length of each strip. This makes an ideal tool for a matching task. The same type of task could be created from scratch using a strip of poster board and stickers, hand-drawn or computer-generated pictures or even rubber-stamped pictures!

TASK:
The student will match box tops to their corresponding bottoms.

MATERIALS:
- ❏ assorted small boxes, covered in self-adhesive paper of different colors
- ❏ a shoebox to hold the loose tops and bottoms
- ❏ a shoebox to hold the assembled boxes

TARGETED SKILLS:
- ❏ matching
- ❏ math readiness
- ❏ motor skills

IDEAS FOR DIFFERENTIATION:

The colored self-adhesive paper makes it easier to match the tops to the bottoms by providing a color cue. For a greater challenge, use the boxes just as they come. Students will be challenged to use only the size of the boxes to determine the appropriate match.

The two shoeboxes could be labeled "open" and "closed" to teach these concepts in relation to the smaller boxes.

TASK:
The student will match objects to photos of the objects.

MATERIALS:
- ❏ various objects and photos of the objects
- ❏ a container to hold the objects
- ❏ a shoebox with dividers inside to create "compartments" to house each object as it is matched
- ❏ photos of each object attached to each compartment

TARGETED SKILLS:
- ❏ matching
- ❏ gross-visual discrimination

IDEAS FOR DIFFERENTIATION:

The task that is pictured is a basic task for students just beginning to match.

To use the same materials as the student progresses through different kinds of visual representation, substitute computer pictures or color drawings for the photos. Once the student can match illustrations to the actual objects, then progress to black and white line drawings. Each step increases the difficulty as the pictures no longer exactly match the objects.

TASK:
The student will match identical, simple pictures.

MATERIALS:
- ❏ 2 sets of identical pictures, one set on a Lotto or Bingo board or other flat surface, the other set loose cards
- ❏ loop-Velcro® on the set of pictures on the board and hook-Velcro® on the backs of the card pictures
- ❏ a container to hold the loose pictures

TARGETED SKILLS:
- ❏ matching
- ❏ visual discrimination
- ❏ pre-reading

IDEAS FOR DIFFERENTIATION:
The same picture board could be used for a more advanced student who has some reading skills. Instead of matching pictures to pictures, a student working on reading could match word cards to the pictures of the words on the board.

SORTING TASKS

TASK:
The student will sort toy cars by color.

MATERIALS:
- ❏ two different-colored toy cars
- ❏ a container such as a sectioned food plate to provide a space for the group of cars to be sorted and a separate space for each color car (or 3 different containers could be used)
- ❏ labels in the bottom of each sorting area

TARGETED SKILLS:
- ❏ sorting
- ❏ pre-math
- ❏ pre-reading

IDEAS FOR DIFFERENTIATION:
The section labels could match the car colors for students who are working on color matching or they could have the color word written in black for students learning to read color words.

Two different types of vehicles could be sorted (e.g., cars and trucks, boats and planes).

TASK:
The student will sort chips by color.

MATERIALS:
- ❏ 3 different-colored poker chips and a small container to hold them
- ❏ 3 cups inserted into 3 holes cut in the top of a shoebox, one cup for each color chip
- ❏ one of each color chip attached to the shoebox lid, above the sorting cups, to label each cup

TARGETED SKILLS:
- ❏ sorting
- ❏ math readiness

IDEAS FOR DIFFERENTIATION:
Some students will be able to sort many colors at a time. A longer shoebox and chips of 5 or 6 colors could be used to expand this task.

Rather than dropping the chips into cups, for greater fine-motor practice, have the student place the chips in slits cut into the top of the box.

TASK:
The student will sort 4 different-colored items by color.

MATERIALS:

❏ manipulatives of 4 different colors (those pictured are leftover pieces from an old game)

❏ a shoebox

❏ a container to hold the loose manipulatives, placed in a hole cut in the top of the shoebox on the left

❏ 4 cups that match the colors of the manipulatives, placed in holes cut in the top of the shoebox on the right

TARGETED SKILLS:

❏ sorting

❏ math readiness

IDEAS FOR DIFFERENTIATION:

If the manipulatives have another distinguishing attribute (such as cars or animals), the task could be expanded to sort by both attributes: red cars, red animals, blue cars, blue animals, green cars, green animals, yellow cars, yellow animals.

TASK:
The student will sort three different colored beads.

MATERIALS:
- ❏ large craft beads in several colors
- ❏ a shoebox
- ❏ a container to hold the beads, placed in a hole cut in the top of the shoebox on the left
- ❏ small containers to hold each color of the sorted beads, placed in holes cut in the top of the shoebox on the right
- ❏ colored pieces of paper to label each of the containers for sorting

TARGETED SKILLS:
- ❏ sorting
- ❏ math readiness

CONSTRUCTION TIP:
If your small containers for the sorted beads don't have a "lip" on them to keep them snugly in the holes, you can use hot glue around the edges of the containers to affix them more permanently to the box.

TASK:
The student will sort colored straws.

MATERIALS:
- ❏ colored drinking straws
- ❏ a container to hold the loose straws
- ❏ a cylindrical container (some potato chip containers work nicely)
- ❏ colored sticker dots to match the straw colors, placed on the lid of the container, with holes punched in each of the dots for the straws

TARGETED SKILLS:
- ❏ sorting
- ❏ math readiness
- ❏ fine-motor

CONSTRUCTION TIP:
In the pictured example, I used a hand-held hole punch to punch holes in the dots on the lid for the straws. You could also cut three holes and color around each hole to match the straw colors if you cannot find stickers that match your straws.

TASK:
The student will sort pictures of boys and girls.

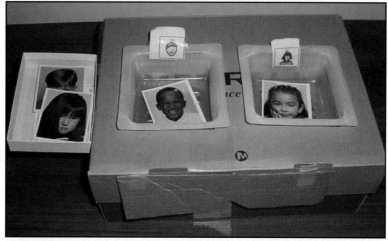

The Picture Communication Symbols ©1981-2005 by Mayer-Johnson LLC. All Rights Reserved Worldwide. Used with permission.

MATERIALS:

❑ index cards with pictures cut from magazines of boys and girls

❑ a container to hold the loose pictures

❑ two containers to hold the sorted pictures, labeled to provide a visual model

❑ a shoebox with holes cut in the top to hold the sorting containers

TARGETED SKILLS:

❑ sorting

❑ visual discrimination

❑ social concept of boys vs. girls

IDEAS FOR DIFFERENTIATION:

Try to include several different examples of boys and girls. Include older boys and girls (men and women) as well. Be certain to use different ethnicities also to ensure appropriate generalization of the concept.

TASK:
The student will sort teddy bears by color.

MATERIALS:
- ❏ 3 different-colored teddy bear counters
- ❏ a container to hold the loose teddy bears
- ❏ a shoebox
- ❏ 3 cups that match the colors of the bears, placed in holes cut in the top of the shoebox

TARGETED SKILLS:
- ❏ sorting
- ❏ math readiness

IDEAS FOR DIFFERENTIATION:
Teddy bear counters sometimes come in different sizes as well as different colors. For a greater challenge, students could sort bears by size and color—big red bears, little red bears, etc. You would need to have another set of colored cups and labels to distinguish the cups for size sorting.

TASK:
The student will sort mini-erasers by category.

MATERIALS:
- ❏ mini erasers
- ❏ a container to hold the erasers
- ❏ a shoebox with smaller containers attached to the top for sorting the erasers
- ❏ a model or other label to identify each cup for sorting

TARGETED SKILLS:
- ❏ sorting
- ❏ math readiness

CONSTRUCTION TIP:
Mini erasers can sometimes be found in dollar stores or other stores where school and office supplies are sold. Another good resource for inexpensive materials like mini erasers in bulk is Oriental Trading Company (1-800-228-2269 or www.orientaltrading.com)

TASK:
The student will sort two different kinds of objects.

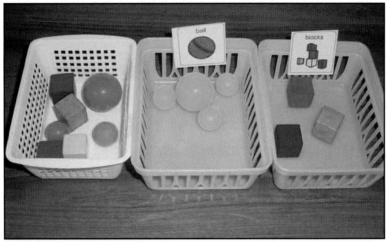

The Picture Communication Symbols ©1981-2005 by Mayer-Johnson LLC. All Rights Reserved Worldwide. Used with permission.

MATERIALS:
❏ several examples of two different types of objects (this example uses blocks and balls)

❏ 3 baskets—one for the mixed objects to be sorted, and one basket for each type of object

❏ labels for the baskets containing each sorted item

TARGETED SKILLS:
❏ sorting

❏ math readiness

❏ reading readiness

IDEAS FOR DIFFERENTIATION:
Beginning learners could sort balls that are identical and blocks that are identical, without having to contend with differences in size and color.

More advanced learners could sort objects or pictures of objects into two categories. For example, the student could sort farm animals and zoo animals; things in the kitchen and things in the bedroom; things used in the summer and things used in the winter, etc.

TASK:
The student will sort two different items and put in the correct slot.

MATERIALS:
- ❏ mini erasers
- ❏ a container to hold the loose erasers
- ❏ a shoebox or other container with two slots cut in the top and labels to identify each slot for sorting

TARGETED SKILLS:
- ❏ sorting
- ❏ math readiness
- ❏ fine-motor

CONSTRUCTION TIP:
Baby wipe containers work nicely as an alternative to shoeboxes. Slots can be cut in the lid with a utility knife and model erasers can be affixed to the lid with hot glue. Mini erasers are a nice size for placing in slots for fine-motor practice.

TASK:
The student will sort two different kinds of objects.

MATERIALS:
- ❏ two kinds of objects to be sorted and a container to hold them
- ❏ two containers for the sorted objects
- ❏ a shoebox with holes cut in the top to hold all of the containers

TARGETED SKILLS:
- ❏ sorting
- ❏ math readiness

IDEAS FOR DIFFERENTIATION:
This task is good for students who need larger materials or more realistic representations of objects. Also, because the objects are larger, fewer items need to be sorted—again, good for beginning level students.

CONSTRUCTION TIP:
The apples and pumpkins pictured above are actually holiday tree ornaments!

TASK:
The student will sort paint samples by color.

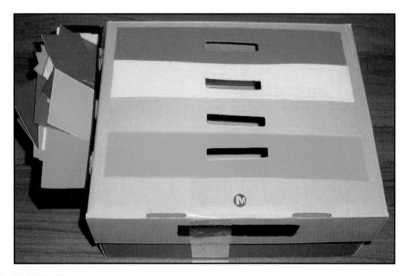

MATERIALS:
- ❏ assorted-colored paint-sample cards or colored paper
- ❏ a small container to hold the loose colored cards
- ❏ a shoebox with slots in the lid, marked with a visual cue for each color to be sorted

TARGETED SKILLS:
- ❏ sorting
- ❏ math readiness

IDEAS FOR DIFFERENTIATION:

Paint-sample cards come in many shades of colors. For an increased challenge and to practice generalization of colors, include many shades of green, red, blue, etc. Students will have to realize that a certain color is a shade of green, even though it may not match the visual cue on the lid exactly.

For beginning students, use one shade for each color and have your model on the lid match the paint-sample shade exactly.

TASK:
The student will sort crayons by color.

MATERIALS:
- ❑ a shoebox with holes cut in the top to hold several containers
- ❑ crayons in a variety of colors
- ❑ a small container to hold the loose crayons, placed in a hole on top of the shoebox
- ❑ smaller containers, one for each color crayon, placed in holes on the right side of the shoebox top

TARGETED SKILLS:
- ❑ sorting
- ❑ math readiness

CONSTRUCTION TIP:
The crayons pictured above are actually crayon erasers. Of course, real crayons could also be used for this task. Use a marker to draw around the rim of each container to match the color crayon to be sorted.

TASK:
The student will sort plastic utensils.

MATERIALS:
- ❏ assorted plastic knives, forks, and spoons
- ❏ a small container to hold the loose utensils
- ❏ a silverware sorter with one of each utensil affixed to the bottom of each section as a model

TARGETED SKILLS:
- ❏ sorting
- ❏ math readiness

CONSTRUCTION TIP:
If you do not have a silverware tray, you can make one by attaching three long jewelry boxes to each other and labeling each box with a knife, fork, and spoon.

TASK:
The student will sort sports cards by category.

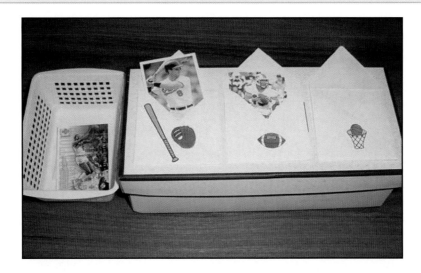

MATERIALS:
- ❑ a shoebox with three small envelopes affixed to the top
- ❑ sports stickers on each envelope to represent baseball, football, and basketball
- ❑ a variety of baseball, football, and basketball sports cards
- ❑ a container to hold the loose cards

TARGETED SKILLS:
- ❑ sorting
- ❑ math readiness
- ❑ visual discrimination

IDEAS FOR DIFFERENTIATION:
Sports cards are a motivator for some students and make interesting task box materials. In addition to the sorting task picture above, sports cards could be used for motor tasks (put in a slot), for matching tasks (match identical cards), for reading tasks (file by the athlete's last name), etc.

TASK:
The student will file index cards by color.

MATERIALS:
❏ a file box with dividers labeled with each color to be sorted

❏ 3x5" index cards, colored with crayons or markers

❏ a small container to hold the loose cards

TARGETED SKILLS:
❏ sorting

❏ math readiness

IDEAS FOR DIFFERENTIATION:
Instead of swatches of color, the index cards could contain pictures of items that are different colors. The student would then look at the picture and file by its color.

For students who read, color words could be written in black on the cards and the student could read the word and file behind the correct color.

TASK:
The student will sort pairs of pictures by determining whether they are the same or different.

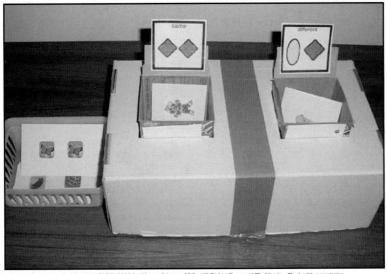

MATERIALS:
- ❏ index cards with two stickers on each card—some cards contain identical stickers, some cards contain two different stickers
- ❏ a container to hold the cards to be sorted
- ❏ a shoebox with two holes cut in the top and two containers placed in the holes, one container labeled "same", the other container labeled "different"

TARGETED SKILLS:
- ❏ visual discrimination
- ❏ matching
- ❏ concept of same and different

IDEAS FOR DIFFERENTIATION:
Other symbols could be programmed on the cards depending on the skill level of the students. Some examples include pairs of numbers, letters, words, shapes, etc.

TASK:
The student will sort items by texture.

MATERIALS:
- ❏ various household items that could be classified as "hard" or "soft" textured
- ❏ a container to hold the items to be sorted
- ❏ a shoebox with two holes cut in the top and two containers placed in the holes, one container labeled "hard," the other container labeled "soft"

TARGETED SKILLS:
- ❏ sorting
- ❏ concept of hard and soft
- ❏ some sensory input

CONSTRUCTION TIP:
Many of the items pictured above were used in other task boxes. Some ideas for materials include: a block, a bell, a plastic cup, a refrigerator magnet, a piece of wood, a pom-pom, a cotton ball, a piece of batting from inside a necklace box, a piece of felt, a feather, a cosmetic sponge, etc.

TASK:
The student will sort pictures by category.

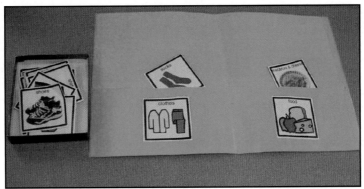

MATERIALS:

❏ pictures of items in two categories (e.g., clothes, food, animals, toys, etc.)

❏ a two-pocket paper folder, with each pocket labeled with one of the categories

❏ a container to hold the loose pictures to be sorted

TARGETED SKILLS:

❏ beginning comprehension

❏ visual discrimination

IDEAS FOR DIFFERENTIATION:

For students who can sort by more complex categories, the task could involve sorting things in the kitchen and things in the bathroom, equipment used for football and equipment used for baseball, winter clothes and summer clothes, etc.

Students who read could sort written words into two categories instead of pictures.

CONSTRUCTION TIP:

Using photo corners on the pockets instead of permanently affixing the category labels will enable this task to be changed to address new categories without making a new folder (see photo of this tip on page xix).

TASK:
The student will sort items by size.

MATERIALS:
❏ blocks of two different lengths, long and short

❏ a container to hold the blocks to be sorted

❏ 2 containers, labeled "long" and "short" for the sorted blocks

TARGETED SKILLS:
❏ visual discrimination

❏ concept of size

IDEAS FOR DIFFERENTIATION:
For students who could sort three ways, long, medium, and short blocks could be used.

The concepts of "big" and "little" could also be practiced in this manner with sets of identical objects—one is big, and one is little.

READING TASKS

TASK:
The student will sequence letters of the alphabet.

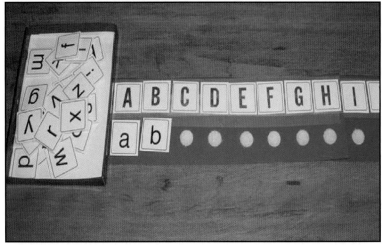

MATERIALS:

❏ two sets of letter cards, one capital and one lowercase

❏ several strips of poster board with one set of letters affixed in a top row and pieces of loop-Velcro® directly under each letter in a bottom row

❏ hook-Velcro® on the backs on each letter card to be matched

❏ a container to hold the loose letter cards

TARGETED SKILLS:

❏ letter recognition

❏ sequencing

❏ pre-reading

IDEAS FOR DIFFERENTIATION:

Some students may need to work on matching capitals to capitals while others could match capitals to lowercase letters.

Students could sequence small groups of letters at a time and master the sequence in segments before joining the entire sequence together. (see tip on page xxi for directions on attaching the strips to extend the sequence)

TASK:
The student will match lowercase to capital letters.

MATERIALS:
- ❏ 3x5" or 4x6" index cards, pre-printed with capital letters, with loop-Velcro® dots to the right of the capital letters
- ❏ smaller cardstock squares, pre-printed with lowercase letters, with hook-Velcro® dots on the backs
- ❏ a piece of cardboard with 26 loop-Velcro® dots for the lowercase letters (this allows the student to view the letters more easily than if they were all collected in a small container since there are so many letters to be matched)
- ❏ 2 baskets—one for the work to be done (capital letter cards) and one for the finished work
- ❏ a tray or box to contain all materials

TARGETED SKILLS:
- ❏ reading readiness
- ❏ letter recognition
- ❏ matching

IDEAS FOR DIFFERENTIATION:
Students could match capital letters to capital letters or lowercase to lowercase.

Students could match letters to a picture that begins with that letter (see task on page 64).

TASK:
The student will match words to identical words.

MATERIALS:
- ❏ a 3-ring binder
- ❏ a plastic sports card holder page, placed in the binder
- ❏ one piece of loop-Velcro® at the top of each of the sports card pockets
- ❏ 2 sets of small cardstock squares with words printed on them—one set has hook-Velcro® on the top of the back of each card and the other set is placed inside each pocket of the sports card holder page
- ❏ strips of loop-Velcro® on one side of the binder to hold the words to be matched

TARGETED SKILLS:
- ❏ matching a sequence of letters
- ❏ reading readiness

CONSTRUCTION TIP:
By placing the loop-Velcro® on the outside of the plastic pockets, the words to be matched can be changed frequently without having to use more loop-Velcro® each time.

TASK:
The student will read words and match to pictures of the word.

MATERIALS:

❏ pictures of food (or any functional pictures of your choosing) with hook-Velcro® on the backs

❏ a small container to hold the loose pictures

❏ a piece of cardboard on which the words of the pictures are written and loop-Velcro® dots are placed beside the words

TARGETED SKILLS:

❏ pre-reading

❏ functional sight

❏ word comprehension

IDEAS FOR DIFFERENTIATION:

For students who are beginning to match words to words, print the word on top of the picture so the written word is available as an additional cue.

Other students may not need the written cue and can match just the picture to the word on the cardboard.

TASK:
The student will read number words and match to sets using clothespins.

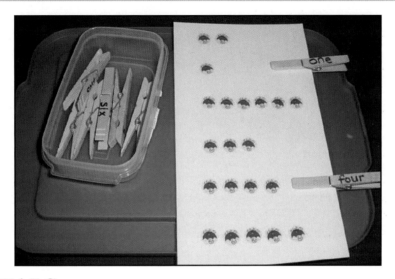

MATERIALS:
- ❏ clothespins with number words written on them
- ❏ a container to hold the loose clothespins
- ❏ small stickers or stamps for making sets
- ❏ a piece of cardboard or poster board with sets of stickers to be counted and matched

TARGETED SKILLS:
- ❏ reading sight words
- ❏ counting sets
- ❏ fine-motor skills to operate clothespins

CONSTRUCTION TIP:
Some students may need visual boundaries to separate the sets. Use a marker to draw lines between the sets to provide a clear distinction.

TASK:
The student will match colored blocks to color words.

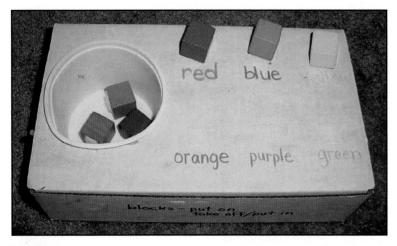

MATERIALS:
- ❏ different colored one-inch blocks
- ❏ a shoebox with a circular hole cut in the left side of the lid and with color words written on the right side of the box
- ❏ a margarine tub or other container to place in the hole in the shoebox to hold the blocks
- ❏ hook-Velcro® pieces placed on the bottom of the blocks and loop-Velcro® pieces placed above the color words on the shoebox lid

TARGETED SKILLS:
- ❏ pre-reading
- ❏ basic sight-word comprehension

IDEAS FOR DIFFERENTIATION:
This shoebox is programmed with color words written in colored magic marker. Students just beginning to learn to read these words can use the color cue to help them identify the correct block.

To program this task without the additional cue, simply write the words in black ink.

TASK:
The student will read color words and match to same colored paperclips.

MATERIALS:
- ❑ a small container of colored paperclips
- ❑ a piece of cardboard or poster board with the color words written on it vertically
- ❑ a container to hold all of the materials

TARGETED SKILLS:
- ❑ pre-reading
- ❑ basic sight-word comprehension
- ❑ fine-motor skills needed to attach paperclips

CONSTRUCTION TIP:
Be sure that you use sturdy cardboard or poster board to make it easier for your student to attach the paperclips. Large paperclips are easier to attach than small ones.

TASK:
The student will read sentences and match the appropriate illustration.

The Picture Communication Symbols ©1981-2005 by Mayer-Johnson LLC. All Rights Reserved Worldwide. Used with permission.

MATERIALS:
- ❏ simple sentences written on a laminated sheet of paper or file folder with small pieces of loop-Velcro® to the left of each sentence
- ❏ pictures that illustrate each sentence with small pieces of hook-Velcro® on the backs
- ❏ a small container to hold the loose pictures

TARGETED SKILLS:
- ❏ beginning reading and reading comprehension

CONSTRUCTION TIP:
The sentences used in this example are:

The girl is sleeping.

The book is red.

The ice is cold.

The sun is yellow.

The snowman has a hat.

TASK:
The student will sort pictures by initial sound.

MATERIALS:
- ❏ an empty baby wipes container (or other container with two separate sides), labeled with the two letter sounds to be identified
- ❏ pictures of items that begin with two different initial consonant sounds (those pictured are cards from an old Memory game without their matches)
- ❏ a small jewelry box or other container to hold the pictures

TARGETED SKILLS:
- ❏ visual discrimination
- ❏ phonemic awareness
- ❏ letter recognition

CONSTRUCTION TIP:
Use Velcro® dots to attach the pictures to the sorting container if students are bothered by pieces that move around or if they tend to play with the pieces. This will also help you assess the student's accuracy even after they have finished the task since the placed pieces will not move.

TASK:
The student will match pictures to their initial letters.

The Picture Communication Symbols ©1981-2005 by Mayer-Johnson LLC. All Rights Reserved Worldwide. Used with permission.

MATERIALS:

❏ 3x5" index cards with a picture representing each letter of the alphabet and loop-Velcro® below each picture

❏ a small container to hold the loose index cards

❏ small squares of cardstock with each letter of the alphabet and hook-Velcro® on the backs

❏ a shoebox for a finished container

❏ rows of loop-Velcro® placed inside a shoebox lid to hold the letter cards

TARGETED SKILLS:

❏ letter recognition

❏ phonemic awareness

IDEAS FOR DIFFERENTIATION:

Uppercase or lowercase letters can be used, depending on the abilities of your students.

Instead of letters, the student could match another picture that starts with the same sound as the one on the cards.

TASK:
The student will identify pictures as characters or settings (people or places).

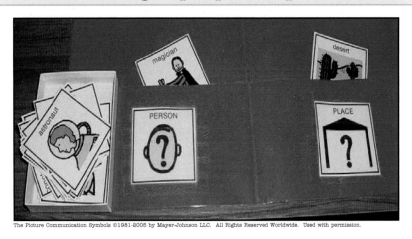

The Picture Communication Symbols ©1981-2005 by Mayer-Johnson LLC. All Rights Reserved Worldwide. Used with permission.

MATERIALS:
- ❏ pictures of people (characters) and pictures of places (settings)
- ❏ a two-pocket paper folder, with the pockets labeled person/place or character/setting
- ❏ a container to hold the loose pictures to be sorted

TARGETED SKILLS:
- ❏ picture identification
- ❏ beginning comprehension
- ❏ sorting

CONSTRUCTION TIP:
Since it may be hard to think of ideas for pictures that students might recognize, here are some suggestions:

PEOPLE		PLACES	
doctor	construction worker	city	post office
Indian	mail carrier	airport	United States
cowboy	police officer	zoo	desert
chef	dentist	circus	beach
firefighter	Abraham Lincoln	North Pole	outer space
soldier	teacher	park	farm

TASK:
The student will sequence a story by what happened first, in the middle, and last.

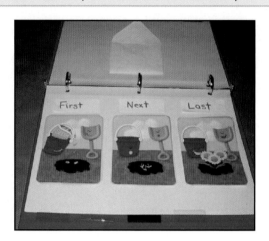

MATERIALS:
- ❏ picture cards that tell a story in sequence with hook-Velcro® on the backs (these can often be purchased in toy stores or where other flashcards are sold; educational supply stores and catalogs carry them as well)
- ❏ a 3-ring binder
- ❏ divider sheets for the binder with plastic tabs on the ends to make finding the next task easier
- ❏ three pieces of loop-Velcro® on the divider sheets under the labels "first," "next," and "last"
- ❏ an envelope on the top side divider sheet to hold the cards to be sequenced

TARGETED SKILLS:
- ❏ attention to detail
- ❏ sequencing
- ❏ comprehension

IDEAS FOR DIFFERENTIATION:
This task could contain one story to be sequenced or a different story could be presented on each divider sheet.

Depending on the abilities of your students, you may wish to use this task as an instructional tool to encourage "re-telling" of the sequenced picture story.

TASK:
The student will file words by first letter.

MATERIALS:

❏ 3x5" cards with various words written on them

❏ a container to hold the 3x5" cards

❏ a 3x5" file box with dividers labeled with each letter of the alphabet

TARGETED SKILLS:

❏ letter identification and recognition

❏ fine-motor skill required for filing

IDEAS FOR DIFFERENTIATION:

It is not necessary for the student to be able to read the word on the card. He only needs to be able to locate the first letter and match it to the same letter in the file box.

To focus attention on the initial letter, you may wish to highlight it, circle it, or write it in a different color.

To create a multi-step task for students who can read the words, have another container that holds pictures that illustrate each word. The student would have to read the word, find its matching picture, and then file it by first letter. The pictures could be attached to the cards with Velcro®.

TASK:
The student will read words and file by category.

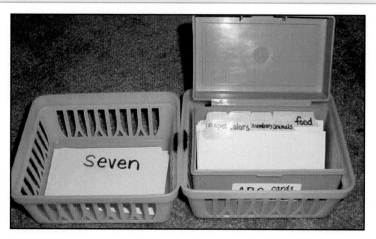

MATERIALS:
- ❏ 3x5" cards with words from several categories written on them (e.g., food words, color words, number words, animal words, etc.)
- ❏ a container to hold the 3x5" cards
- ❏ a 3x5" file box with dividers labeled with each of the categories on the cards (i.e., dividers say "food," "colors," "numbers," etc.)

TARGETED SKILLS:
- ❏ sight word reading
- ❏ comprehension
- ❏ categorization
- ❏ fine-motor skill required for filing

CONSTRUCTION TIP:
You can "recycle" these word cards for use with several different types of tasks. For example, this photo shows the initial letter written in red and the rest of the word written in black. A child working on filing by initial letter could use this same set of cards with alphabetical dividers and file each word by the first letter that is highlighted in red.

The cards could also be used to focus on comprehension. If Velcro® dots are attached to the card beneath the word, students could match a picture that illustrates the word to the written word to demonstrate their understanding.

TASK:
The student will place words in alphabetical order.

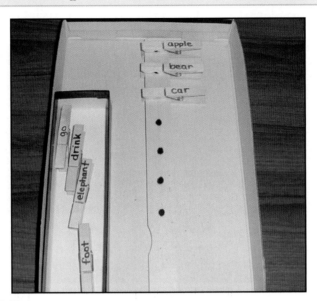

MATERIALS:
- ❑ clothespins, with various words written on them, each beginning with a different letter
- ❑ a container to hold the loose clothespins
- ❑ a paint stirring stick or a sturdy piece of cardboard, with markings for a visual cue for clothespin placement
- ❑ a shoebox lid or other tray to contain all items

TARGETED SKILLS:
- ❑ letter identification
- ❑ letter sequencing
- ❑ fine-motor skill required for operating clothespins

IDEAS FOR DIFFERENTIATION:
You can make this task as difficult as you need to based on the words you write on the clothespins. Students who are just beginning to sequence letters can use words that each start with a different letter, in sequence (A-F, for example), as shown in the pictured task. Other students could sequence words by first letter, with some letters in the alphabet missing (for example, words that start with A, C, G, K, M, T, Z). Students who are significantly more advanced could alphabetize by the second or third letters.

TASK:
The student will read different months and match to the corresponding holiday.

The Picture Communication Symbols ©1981-2005 by Mayer-Johnson LLC. All Rights Reserved Worldwide. Used with permission.

MATERIALS:
- ❏ a 3-ring binder with loop-Velcro® strips on the bottom portion of each binder side
- ❏ 4x6" or 5x8" cards (depending on the size of your binder), preprogrammed with the name of each month of the year, with a piece of loop-Velcro® underneath each month name
- ❏ picture symbols that depict various holidays, with hook-Velcro® on the backs

TARGETED SKILLS:
- ❏ functional reading
- ❏ comprehension

IDEAS FOR DIFFERENTIATION:
For more advanced readers, the index cards could contain a sentence to be completed by the name of the holiday. For example, the card could read "In February, we celebrate_____." The choices at the bottom of the binder could be the word names of each holiday, without the picture cues.

TASK:
The student will read words and match them to their opposite.

MATERIALS:

❏ a 3-ring binder with 2 rows of loop-Velcro® strips on the bottom portion of each binder side

❏ 4x6" or 5x8" cards (depending on the size of your binder), preprogrammed with one word of an opposite pair, with loop-Velcro® on the back of each card

❏ one extra card that is blank on the front but has loop-Velcro® on the back (to be used for the opposite of the first word)

❏ strips of cardstock with the second word in each opposite pair and hook-Velcro® on the back of each word strip

TARGETED SKILLS:

❏ functional reading

❏ comprehension

❏ concept of opposites

IDEAS FOR DIFFERENTIATION:

Picture cues may help some students understand the concept of opposites and could be substituted for the written words, especially for students who are not yet reading.

WRITING
TASKS

TASK:
The student will trace lines.

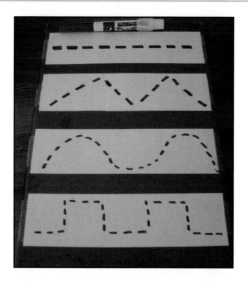

MATERIALS:

❑ a shoebox with different kinds of dotted lines drawn on the top

❑ clear, self-adhesive paper to cover the lid of the shoebox

❑ a dry-erase marker, attached to the top of the box with Velcro®

TARGETED SKILLS:

❑ tracing lines

❑ eye-hand coordination

IDEAS FOR DIFFERENTIATION:

For students who have difficulty tracing dotted lines, you can use a highlighter or other light colored marker to draw solid lines on the box before covering the lid. The student can then use a dark marker and trace the light, solid line. Sometimes this is easier visually.

CONSTRUCTION TIP:

Covering the lid in self-adhesive paper allows a dry-erase marker to be used and then erased so that the box can be used over and over.

TASK:
The student will draw lines to match.

MATERIALS:
- ❏ two sets of identical stickers
- ❏ a shoebox with the stickers on top in two vertical rows, one set of stickers in each row
- ❏ clear, self-adhesive paper to cover the lid of the shoebox
- ❏ a dry-erase marker, attached to the top of the box with Velcro®

TARGETED SKILLS:
- ❏ visual discrimination
- ❏ matching
- ❏ drawing lines
- ❏ eye-hand coordination

IDEAS FOR DIFFERENTIATION:
To make this task easier, place the stickers in the same order in both columns so the student only has to draw a straight, horizontal line.

For students who are not yet able to draw lines independently, dotted lines could be preprogrammed on the lid of the box (in different colors for visual clarity) and the student could trace the lines.

TASK:
The student will spell his or her name in sequence.

The Picture Communication Symbols ©1981-2005 by Mayer-Johnson LLC. All Rights Reserved Worldwide. Used with permission.

MATERIALS:
- ❏ small cards with letters of the child's name printed on them and with hook-Velcro® on the back
- ❏ a container to hold the loose letters
- ❏ a spelling model with the child's name printed in individual letters on the top and with loop-Velcro® underneath each letter

TARGETED SKILLS:
- ❏ spelling
- ❏ letter recognition and matching

IDEAS FOR DIFFERENTIATION:
This task can be used for several stages of spelling. Initially, the child can match each letter of his or her name. As the child becomes proficient with matching, you can cover a few of the letters with a small Post-It note to hide the letters from view. As the child masters this stage, all the letters can be covered and the child can spell his name without any visual model.

TASK:
The student will match letters to spell words.

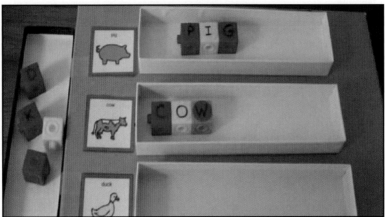

The Picture Communication Symbols ©1981-2006 by Mayer-Johnson LLC. All Rights Reserved Worldwide. Used with permission.

MATERIALS:
- ❏ a shoebox and 4 smaller containers—one container attached to the left side of the shoebox and three attached to the top
- ❏ pictures with the words written above to be used as models, affixed to the left of each of the containers on top of the shoebox
- ❏ linking letters or linking blocks with letters on them

TARGETED SKILLS:
- ❏ spelling
- ❏ letter recognition and matching
- ❏ fine-motor

CONSTRUCTION TIP:
If linking letters are not available, you can use linking blocks. Those pictured above have colored dot stickers placed on them and the letters have been written on the dots. If neither of these options is available, you could print letters on squares of cardstock with hook-Velcro® on the back. If you place a strip of loop-Velcro® inside each of the boxes on top of the shoebox, the student can stick the cardstock letters in sequence on each strip of Velcro®.

TASK:
The student will spell words by matching letters on clothespins.

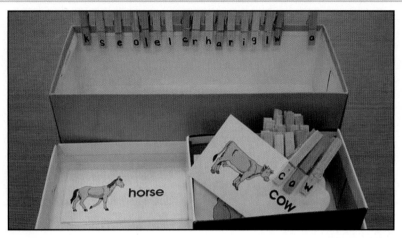

MATERIALS:

❏ cards with pictures and words (sets of word-picture cards can be purchased at many teacher stores or you can make your own)

❏ a container to hold the loose cards

❏ clothespins preprogrammed with the individual letters needed to spell the words on the cards

❏ a shoebox or other long, upright surface to attach the clothespins for easy viewing by students

❏ a container in which to place the completed cards with clothespins attached

TARGETED SKILLS:

❏ spelling

❏ letter recognition and matching

❏ beginning sight-word exposure

❏ fine-motor skills required to operate clothespins

IDEAS FOR DIFFERENTIATION:

For students who can spell from memory, use the same idea but omit the written word on the card. Students can use the clothespins to spell the word pictured on the card without the matching prompt.

TASK:
The student will construct a simple sentence using pictures and a prompt card.

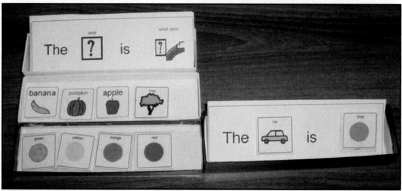

The Picture Communication Symbols ©1981-2005 by Mayer-Johnson LLC. All Rights Reserved Worldwide. Used with permission.

MATERIALS:
- ❏ several sentence prompt cards that say "The _____ (what?) is _____ (what color?)."
- ❏ loop-Velcro® pieces on each prompt card in the two spots to be filled in by the student
- ❏ pictures of objects that are clearly a certain color, with hook-Velcro® on the backs
- ❏ pictures of colors (that correspond to the objects), with hook-Velcro® on the backs
- ❏ four small containers: one for the sentence prompts, one for the object pictures, one for the color pictures, and one for the completed sentences

TARGETED SKILLS:
- ❏ sentence construction
- ❏ color recognition and identification

IDEAS FOR DIFFERENTIATION:
Students may be able to build the entire sentence, including "the" and "is". This may be the next step for some students after mastering this task as it is pictured.

TASK:
The student will construct a simple sentence using word cards.

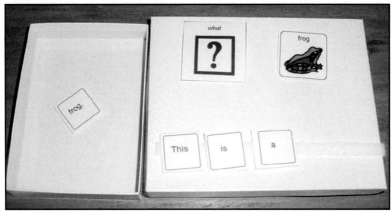

The Picture Communication Symbols ©1981-2005 by Mayer-Johnson LLC. All Rights Reserved Worldwide. Used with permission.

MATERIALS:

❏ a shoebox with a picture affixed to the top and a strip of loop-Velcro® underneath the picture

❏ preprinted cards with individual sight words that construct a simple sentence

❏ hook-Velcro® on the backs of the word cards

❏ a container to hold the loose word cards

TARGETED SKILLS:

❏ sight-word recognition

❏ sentence construction

IDEAS FOR DIFFERENTIATION:

Students may construct longer sentences by adding descriptive words such as quantity and color words. (For example, "I see one green frog.")

MATH
TASKS

TASK:
The student will demonstrate one-to-one correspondence by placing one peg in each spot.

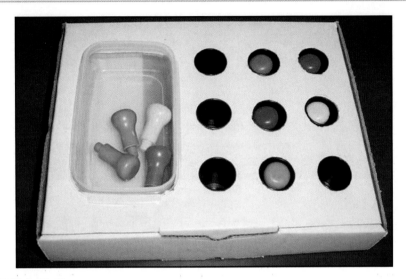

MATERIALS:
- ❑ plastic pegs
- ❑ small container to hold the pegs
- ❑ empty film canisters or other small cup-like containers
- ❑ shoebox with holes cut in the top for the film canisters and a larger hole for the container of pegs

TARGETED SKILLS:
- ❑ one-to-one correspondence
- ❑ math readiness

CONSTRUCTION TIP:
To create the holes for the film canisters, it is sometimes easier to trace the bottom of the containers on the top of the box and then cut X's in the box rather than cutting a circular hole. The canisters can be pushed through the X's and will be held snugly in place.

TASK:
The student will demonstrate one-to-one correspondence by placing one cotton ball in each spot in an ice cube tray.

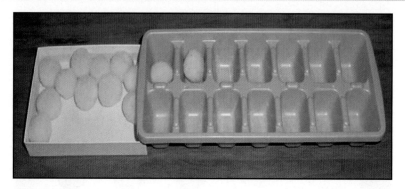

MATERIALS:
❏ cotton balls

❏ small container to hold the cotton balls

❏ empty ice cube tray

TARGETED SKILLS:
❏ one-to-one correspondence

❏ math readiness

IDEAS FOR DIFFERENTIATION:
To embed fine-motor practice into this task, provide tongs or tweezers to be used to pick up and place each cotton ball in the tray.

CONSTRUCTION TIP:
To create a model to show how the task is to be completed, you may wish to place one cotton ball permanently in one of the ice spots. You could affix the cotton ball with hot glue, or you could simply put the cotton ball in the tray and place Scotch tape over the opening so that the cotton ball cannot be removed.

TASK:
The student will count dots and match to the corresponding numeral.

MATERIALS:
- ❏ index cards with sets from 1-10 using dot stickers, with loop-Velcro® on the bottom of each card
- ❏ a container to hold the loose cards
- ❏ small squares of cardstock preprinted with the numerals 1-10, with hook-Velcro® on the back
- ❏ a container to hold the loose numbers
- ❏ a container to hold the finished cards
- ❏ a shoebox or other tray to contain all materials

TARGET SKILLS:
- ❏ counting
- ❏ number recognition
- ❏ 1:1 correspondence

IDEAS FOR DIFFERENTIATION:
For students who are just beginning to count sets, the index cards could contain sets of 1 or 2 only, with multiple examples of each. Students would then either match a 1 or a 2 to each card, focusing only on these two numerals.

TASK:
The student will count sets from 1-10 and match the correct numeral to the set.

The Picture Communication Symbols ©1981-2005 by Mayer-Johnson LLC.
All Rights Reserved Worldwide. Used with permission.

MATERIALS:
- ❑ small squares of cardstock preprinted with the numerals 1-10, with hook-Velcro® on the back
- ❑ a flat container with two loop-Velcro® strips for placing the numeral choices
- ❑ 4x6" or 5x8" unlined index cards preprinted with pictures of items in groups from 1-10 (a different set on each card); a small piece of loop-velcro® on each card to the right of the group of pictures
- ❑ a container to hold the cards to be completed
- ❑ a container to hold the finished cards
- ❑ a tray to hold all materials

TARGET SKILLS:
- ❑ counting
- ❑ number recognition
- ❑ 1:1 correspondence

IDEAS FOR DIFFERENTIATION:
For students working on basic computation skills of addition or subtraction, the task could be designed with two sets of items (for adding or subtracting). The student would then perform the computation and place the numeral of the answer on the card.

TASK:
The student will sequence numbers.

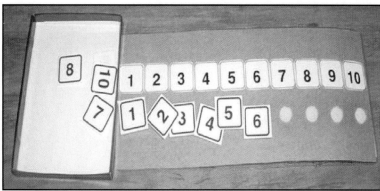

The Picture Communication Symbols ©1981-2005 by Mayer-Johnson LLC. All Rights Reserved Worldwide. Used with permission.

MATERIALS:

❏ cardboard or poster board with pieces of loop-Velcro® in a horizontal row

❏ numbers attached to the cardboard or poster board to serve as a model

❏ small squares of cardstock with pre-printed numbers (or you can use number stickers) with hook-Velcro® on the back

❏ container for numbers

TARGET SKILLS:

❏ number sense

❏ number recognition

❏ sequencing

IDEAS FOR DIFFERENTIATION:

For differing tasks, students could sequence the numbers 1-10, 11-20, or 1-20. Make two separate strips that can be joined at the ends with Velcro® to extend the sequence (see a photo of this tip on page xxi).

Students could practice skip counting by sequencing numbers by 2's, 5's, 10's, etc.

The attached numbers can be covered with Post-It notes when students no longer need to rely on the visual model.

TASK:
The student will make sets on a box.

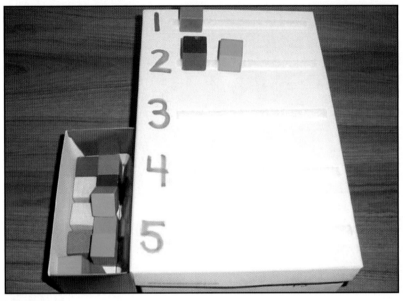

MATERIALS:
- ❏ a shoebox with the numbers 1-5 written vertically on the left side of the lid
- ❏ strips of loop-Velcro® placed next to each number on the lid
- ❏ manipulative items, with hook-Velcro® on each bottom
- ❏ a small container to hold the manipulatives

TARGET SKILLS:
- ❏ counting
- ❏ number recognition

IDEAS FOR DIFFERENTIATION:
For students who need a visual cue in order to make the sets correctly, individual pieces of Velcro® could be placed next to the numbers. The student would then place each block on a piece of Velcro® using one-to-one correspondence to make the sets.

TASK:
The student will fill in the missing numerals in a sequence.

MATERIALS:
- ❏ cardboard with 20 pieces of loop-Velcro® in two rows
- ❏ small squares of cardstock pre-printed with the missing numbers with hook-Velcro® on the back
- ❏ container for numbers

TARGET SKILLS:
- ❏ number sense
- ❏ number recognition
- ❏ sequencing

CONSTRUCTION TIP:
Present the task to the student with some numbers already on the board. You could permanently affix some of the numbers to the board, but that does not allow for the task to be changed. If you attach a piece of Velcro® for each number, you can change the task each time you present it, showing the student different numbers already in sequence.

TASK:
The student will sequence numbers by skip counting.

MATERIALS:
- ❏ a shoebox with pieces of loop-Velcro® in a row on top
- ❏ small squares of cardstock with pre-printed numbers (or you can use calendar shapes as pictured) with hook-Velcro® on the back
- ❏ a container to hold the loose number cards

TARGET SKILLS:
- ❏ number sense
- ❏ number recognition
- ❏ sequencing
- ❏ counting by 5

IDEAS FOR DIFFERENTIATION:
To have students practice skip counting by 2s, 5s and 10s all on the same box, simply use three different shapes and create three rows of Velcro® on the box. Program one shape with multiples of 2, a different shape with multiples of 5, and still another shape with multiples of 10. You could also use different color cards if shapes are not available. Be sure to place the first number of each sequence on the box to serve as a model since there will be so many manipulatives to work with.

TASK:
The student will seriate items by size.

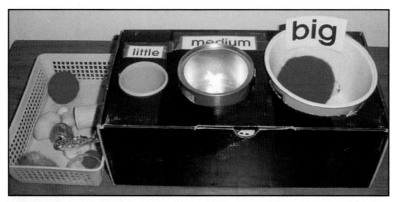

MATERIALS:
- ❏ three containers placed inside holes in a shoebox—one small, one medium, and one large
- ❏ labels for each container that say "little," "medium," and "big" or "small," "medium," and "large," depending on your preference
- ❏ items that come in three sizes
- ❏ a container to hold all of the loose items

TARGET SKILLS:
- ❏ concept of size
- ❏ beginning reading

CONSTRUCTION TIP:
You could purchase a commercial size-sorting package from an educational supply store, or you could assemble items of different sizes from around the house. Some ideas include:
- ❏ bite-sized, regular-sized, and jumbo candy bars
- ❏ pencils of various lengths (a stub, one that is half gone, and a brand new pencil)
- ❏ child-sized, regular-sized, and serving-sized spoons
- ❏ 3 different-sized toothbrushes

Many craft store items come in different sizes, too (e.g., pom-poms, bells, feathers, wooden spools, etc.).

TASK:
The student will make sets of items from 1-3.

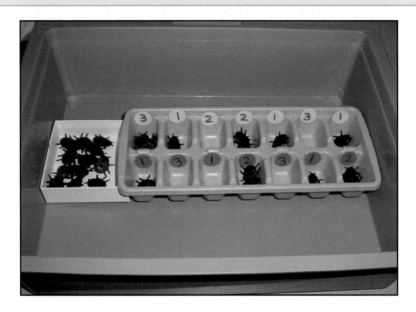

MATERIALS:
❏ small items for manipulatives
❏ a container for the manipulatives
❏ an ice tray or egg carton, with each spot labeled 1,2, or 3
❏ a tray to contain all materials

TARGET SKILLS:
❏ counting
❏ number sense
❏ number recognition
❏ making sets

IDEAS FOR DIFFERENTIATION:
Students could use pennies or other coin combinations to place the correct amount of money (as labeled .37, for example) in each spot.

Students could work on one to one correspondence by placing only one item in each spot.

TASK:
The student will make sets of items to 10.

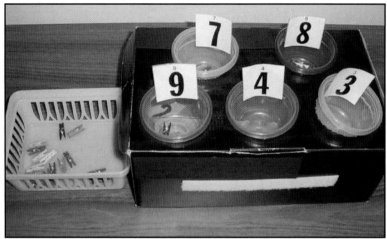

The Picture Communication Symbols ©1981-2005 by Mayer-Johnson LLC. All Rights Reserved Worldwide. Used with permission.

MATERIALS:

❏ small items for manipulatives

❏ a container for the manipulatives

❏ a shoebox with several holes cut in the top and small containers in each of the holes

❏ labels for each small container to show the set to be made

TARGET SKILLS:

❏ counting

❏ number sense

❏ number recognition

❏ making sets

CONSTRUCTION TIP:

If you attach the number labels to each container with Velcro®, the numbers can be changed easily to vary the task.

TASK:
The student will extend a pattern.

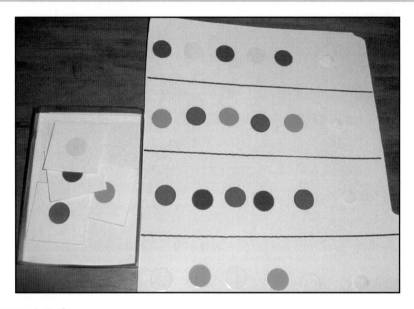

MATERIALS:

- ❏ colored dots placed in a pattern, leaving the last one empty
- ❏ one piece of loop-Velcro® in the place of the last pattern element
- ❏ loose colored dots on cardstock that complete each of the patterns
- ❏ hook-Velcro® on the back of the loose dot cards
- ❏ a small container to hold the loose cards

TARGET SKILLS:

- ❏ pattern recognition and extension

CONSTRUCTION TIP:

Not all task boxes have to be boxes. In this case, one side of a file folder is used to display the work to be completed. However, with this task, a whole file folder could also be used to contain all pieces of the task: the loose cards could be in an envelope attached to the left side of the folder and the patterns to be completed could still be on the right.

APPENDIX I: IEP GOALS

As with all good instruction, the use of task boxes is intended to address specific areas of need as identified in a student's Individual Education Plan (IEP). Goals should be customized to address each student's present levels of performance, the conditions under which the skill will be addressed, and the targeted level of mastery. Listed below are several ideas for reflecting a student's need to learn to work independently and to achieve a variety of skills.

Goals related to using a work system independently:

❏ The student will use a schedule to complete a series of independent work tasks.

❏ The student will follow an established system for "finished" work (putting it in a basket, back on the shelf, etc.).

❏ The student will work independently for _____ minutes.

Goals related to motor tasks:

❏ The student will complete tasks involving pulling objects off a fixed structure and placing them in a container.

❏ The student will complete tasks involving placing one item at a time through a small slot.

❏ The student will complete tasks using a pincer grasp to remove clothespins or other small items.

❏ The student will complete a two-step motor task to assemble an item.

❏ The student will build a structure using interlocking blocks.

Goals related to matching or sorting tasks:

❏ The student will identify items as same or different.

❏ The student will match items that are the same color.

❏ The student will sort items by color.

❏ The student will match items that are the same size.

❏ The student will sort items by size.

❏ The student will match items that are the same shape.

❏ The student will sort items by shape.

❏ The student will match identical items or pictures.

❏ The student will sort items by category (animals, people, cars, etc.).

Goals related to reading tasks:

❏ The student will match same-case letters.

❏ The student will match uppercase to lowercase letters.

❏ The student will sequence letters of the alphabet.

❏ The student will match words.

❏ The student will match words to pictures of the same words.

❏ The student will match pictures to sentences describing the pictures.

❏ The student will match pictures to the letter of its initial sound.

❏ The student will sort characters and settings (in picture or word form).

❏ The student will sequence a 3-part story using pictures.

❏ The student will sort words by category.

❏ The student will match the opposite word to a given word.

❏ The student will place words in alphabetical order by first letter.

Goals related to writing tasks:

❏ The student will trace straight and curved lines.

❏ The student will draw lines to match identical items.

❏ The student will sequence the letters of his or her first name.

❏ The student will match letters to spell a given word.

❏ The student will construct a simple sentence placing pictures in the correct order.

❏ The student will construct a simple sentence by placing words in the correct order.

Goals related to math tasks:

❏ The student will demonstrate one-to-one correspondence by placing one item in a corresponding container.

❏ The student will count sets and match the correct numeral to the set.

❏ The student will sequence numerals.

❏ The student will make sets to match given numerals.

❏ The student will fill in the missing numeral in a sequence.

❏ The student will sequence numerals by skip counting by _____.

❏ The student will seriate items by size.

❏ The student will extend _____ patterns. (AB, AAB, etc.)

APPENDIX II:
DATA SHEETS

DATA SHEET: MOTOR TASKS

Student_____   Date____/____/____

Level and % Correct	L	%	L	%	L	%	L	%
Put blocks in slot								
Pull clothespins off box, put in hole								
Put mini balls in hole								
Pull blocks off box, put in hole								
Pull teddy bears off box								
Put big checkers in slot								
Park cars in spot								
Assemble film canisters and drop in slot								
Put poker chips in slot								
Put coins in bank								
Put facial features on a potato toy								
Block construction								

Independence Level codes:
I = independent   PA = partial assistance   MA = maximal assistance

DATA SHEET: MATCHING TASKS

Student_____   Date_____/_____/_____

Level and % Correct	L	%	L	%	L	%	L	%
Plastic egg color match								
Clothespin color match								
Puzzle piece outline match								
Blocks color match								
Tile sample color match								
Simple picture match								
Match block pattern								
Memory match								
Shape match								
Border picture match								
Box top match								
Object to photo match								
Lotto picture match								

Independence Level codes:
I = independent   PA = partial assistance   MA = maximal assistance

DATA SHEET: SORTING TASKS

Student_____ Date____/____/____

Level and % Correct	L	%	L	%	L	%	L	%
2-color car sort								
3-color poker chip sort								
4-color game piece sort								
3-way colored beads sort								
Colored straw sort								
Boy-girl sort								
Teddy bear color sort								
Sports eraser sort								
Balls and blocks sort								
Ghosts and pumpkins sort								
Apples and pumpkins sort								
Paint card sort								
Crayon sort								
Plastic utensils sort								
Sort sports cards by category								
File index cards by color								
Same/different sort								
Texture sort								
Category sort								
Sort by size								

Independence Level codes:
I = independent   PA = partial assistance   MA = maximal assistance

DATA SHEET: READING TASKS

Student_____ Date_____/_____/_____

Level and % Correct	L	%	L	%	L	%	L	%
Alphabet sequence								
Upper- to lower-case letter match								
Word-to-word match								
Word-to-picture match								
Clothespin word-to-picture match								
Blocks-to-color words match								
Paperclips-to-color words match								
Sentence-to-picture match								
Initial sound sort								
Initial letter match								
Character and setting sort								
3-part story sequence								
File by first letter								
File words by category								
Alphabetical order on clothespins								
Holiday-to-month name binder								
Opposites binder								

Independence Level codes:

I = independent   PA = partial assistance   MA = maximal assistance

DATA SHEET: WRITING TASKS

Student_____ Date_____/_____/_____

Level and % Correct	L	%	L	%	L	%	L	%
Trace lines								
Draw lines to match								
Spell name sequence								
Letter match to spell word								
Attach clothespins to spell words								
Simple sentence construction with pictures								
Simple sentence construction with words								

Independence Level codes:
I = independent   PA = partial assistance   MA = maximal assistance

DATA SHEET: MATH TASKS

Student_____ Date_____/_____/_____

Level and % Correct	L	%	L	%	L	%	L	%
1:1 correspondence with pegs and film canisters								
1:1 correspondence with cotton balls and ice cube tray								
Count dots, match to number								
Count sets of items, match to number								
Sequence numbers on strip								
Make sets on a box								
Fill in the sequence with missing number								
Sequence by skip counting								
Size seriation								
Make sets in ice cube tray								
Make sets in cups								
Extend pattern with stickers								

Independence Level codes:

I = independent   PA = partial assistance   MA = maximal assistance